# EXMOOR IN SIGHT

*setting the scene*

## MICHAEL DEERING

**EXMOOR BOOKS**

First published in 1997 by Exmoor Books

SPECIAL NOTICE
Every effort has been made to obtain the permission of all owners and copyright
holders of material reproduced in this book.  Should any have been overlooked or
omitted or in the event of any other query please contact the publisher.

The views expressed in this book are those of the author and are not necessarily
those of the Exmoor National Park Authority.

**British Library Cataloguing in Publication Data**
A CIP catalogue record for this book is available from The British Library

ISBN 0 86183 320 1

EXMOOR BOOKS
Dulverton, Somerset

Trade sales enquiries:
HALSGROVE
Halsgrove House
Lower Moor Way
Tiverton EX16 6SS
Tele: 01884 243242
Fax: 01884 243325

Exmoor Books is a partnership between The Exmoor Press and The Exmoor National Park Authority.

Printed in Great Britain by Hillman Printers (Frome) Ltd.

# ⤙ CONTENTS ⤚

# ⊷ INTRODUCTION ⊷

Much of the history of Exmoor has been written down and recorded in books often illustrated with old photographs, but never before has there been an attempt to make a comprehensive pictorial record. Photography, as we know it today, was discovered in 1839 and from that time on it has been possible to make a permanent visual record of a moment in time.

Today there are few households that do not possess a camera and most of us have an album, a drawer or a box in which we keep the photographs of our home and family in picture form. Indeed when we go on holiday taking the camera is a must. We like to record how we journeyed, where we stayed and the places we went to, ourselves and our companions. Then, from time to time in years to come, we find the pictures, refresh our memories and with some glee show our grown up children all those early, so embarrassing pictures of themselves when very little.

This was not always so. It was some fifty years after the discovery of photography that the earliest pictures we have found of Exmoor were taken. This was the time when Mr Eastman, the founder of Kodak, introduced roll film and a simple camera, the No 1 Kodak, in which it could be used. Some of the pictures in this book were copied from the 2 $1/2$ inch (6 cm) square prints from photographs taken with the No 1 Kodak. It was a costly hobby and few could afford it. The camera cost five guineas and the developing and printing two guineas. A guinea was 21/- (£1.05), more than a week's wages for most at that time. Within a few years though, the Pocket Kodak was marketed at only one guinea and a twelve exposure roll film cost only two shillings to develop and print, making photography much more affordable. This little camera took pictures 2 x $1^1/_2$ inch (5 x 4 cm) in size and dozens of the pictures in the Archive have been reproduced from these small prints. The professional photographer kept to his glass negatives which had the advantage over flexible roll film, when used in the design of the camera of the day, of being absolutely flat, thus giving far better definition. Unfortunately very few of these survive – but what quality!

For these reasons this photographic history is necessarily limited to the last 120 years or so but also included are copies of paintings and black and white sketches made in earlier times when the world was dependent on the artist with his brush or pen and pencil to make visual records. So within this book are a multitude of pictures bringing vividly to our eyes the way of life of our forefathers in all its aspects together with more contemporary photographs showing innovation and change. Many of the pictures are from family albums and have not previously been published.

# ⊶ PREFACE ⊷

All the pictures in this book can be found in the Exmoor Photographic Archive. The author during his some twenty years of photography on Exmoor realised that although there was much written work on the area there was no comprehensive pictorial record. Having much material available himself he decided to embark on an historical archive that would ultimately be useful for education, the general public interest and the Exmoor National Park Authority itself.

The Archive is presently housed in the Heritage Centre in the Guildhall Centre in Dulverton where it is available for viewing by anyone. It is hoped that the Exmoor National Park Authority will welcome its incorporation into the Exmoor Resource Centre which we understand it is hoping to create.

The Archive is an on-going project bringing together copies of photographs taken within and adjacent to the geographical area contained by the boundaries of Exmoor National Park. The photographs in the Archive date from the 1870s (the earliest found) to the present day. The pictures chosen illustrate the changes, if any, that have occurred over the last century, to the landscape, to settlements and buildings, to schools and churches, to farming, to crafts and trades, to transport, and to sport, recreation and tourism. The collection is catalogued in such a way that pictures of these and many other subjects may easily be searched.

Over 1600 pictures have been borrowed, copied, and catalogued filling some 36 albums. This first volume of *Exmoor in Sight* is a brief selection of pictures from the Archive, which, with simple text written to encourage question and discussion, sets the scene. More pictures of some of the areas covered in this volume and more subjects, for example, crafts, trades and transport will be illustrated in subsequent volumes.

(The author would be very pleased to hear from anyone with more pictures or information to add to the Archive.)

# ⤙ ACKNOWLEDGEMENTS ⤚

Without all the pictures lent to me for copying and inclusion in the Exmoor Photographic Archive it would have been impossible to produce this book. In addition to contributions from over 120 individuals, the Lyn Museum at Lynton, the Porlock Museum, the West Somerset Museum of Rural Life at Allerford, the Exmoor Horn Sheep Society, the Exmoor National Park Authority and the Exmoor Society have all contributed to the Archive.

Brian Pearce of Exmoor National Park Authority deserves a special vote of thanks for his help in identifying and dating the photographs in the Archive. Brian has walked every part of the moor and has an encyclopaedic memory of nearly every view. Thanks also to Hilary Binding for her careful and constructive editing and to Karen Binaccioni for her careful preparation of the pictures and script.

In this volume of *Exmoor in Sight* I know I have used pictures contributed by Miss May Acland from her family albums, by Mr and Mrs Ball from their history of Wootton Courtenay, by Anne Le Bas, James Bingley, and J. F. Bruford; from Mr and Mrs R. Chown and Stan Curtis; from the family albums of Sir Robin Dunn and Mrs M. Elliott; from the German family of Dulverton; from David Head, David Hunt, Frances Jenkins, Florence Hall and the Lion Hotel, Dulverton; family pictures from the Very Rev. Canon Frederick Smyth, Christine Taylor and Lionel Wilkins and memories of living in Oldways End by Frank Summers as well as pictures from museums, societies and the Exmoor National Park Authority. There will be others I would thank if I knew who they were.

Thanks are due too from all of us to the professional photographers Messrs Catford, Frith, German, Hole and Vowles and many others, long gone, without whom many of these moments in time would not have been recorded.

My wife Norma has given me continuous encouragement not only in writing this book but also to my devoting so much time and money to the production and continuity of the Archive. She also possesses the quite infuriating ability to home in on the one spelling mistake or grammatical error hidden in the middle of an A4 sheet of paper – the one I was sure I had not made! – I always say thanks.

· Michael Deering
March 1997

# ⊰ INDEX TO ILLUSTRATIONS ⊱

Pictures taken in the Exmoor parishes listed below appear on the page numbers shown against each parish. The Archive is based on civil not ecclesiastical parishes. Some of these civil parishes have now been amalgamated. By the time all the volumes of *Exmoor in Sight* have been published it is hoped that all 42 parishes will be represented but this will depend entirely on contributions to the Archive. There are, at the time of writing, no pictures of Elworthy, High Bray, Kentisbury, Skilgate or Twitchen in the Archive. Pictures from 26 of the parishes are included in this first volume.

* Minehead is outside the boundary of Exmoor National Park but like Brushford, Watchet and Williton is included in the Archive because of its close association with the Park.

*The Parishes of Exmoor.*

# SECTION ONE
# *People and Places*

*Dulverton 133 1904. Looking down Bridge Street towards the Bridge. Busy, but not a car anywhere!*

The first professional photographers on Exmoor, men like Herbert Hole of Williton and John German of Dulverton, were working during the last decades of the nineteenth century, round about the same time that the coming of the railways and the introduction of machinery began to change the lives of the people who lived in what is now Exmoor National Park. Visual records of themselves, their families and homes had always been the prerogative of the wealthy, the landowners and the gentry by way of artists with brush or pen. This was an expensive business quite out of reach of the pocket of the ordinary working man – indeed he would have been thought by his betters to be thoroughly presumptuous to even contemplate such a thing.

Then along came this new-fangled photography and, on a family occasion, a wedding, an anniversary or a special event, it became possible, indeed desirable, to have a photograph taken, only black and white admittedly, but one got a picture recording accurately and in detail that moment in time. It was affordable – and it was possible to have copies made.

*Wootton Courtenay 29 1926. The village carpenter and his wife, Mr and Mrs James Morgan, a picture probably taken to mark a special occasion. We know that the photograph was taken in 1926 although their costume is that of the early 1900s. In the life they led there would have been little need for formal clothes and the ones they are wearing were quite likely to have been carefully kept from early on in their married life to be worn on special occasions. Perhaps Mr Morgan wears his wedding suit made by the village tailor. Dating photographs can be difficult as the remote rural areas were often twenty years behind the times compared to urban areas.*

Exmoor is even now a remote, perhaps mysterious, part of England: a place that attracts the explorer in us. Before the coming of the railway train such exploration could only be done by those who could afford to own or hire a horse drawn carriage or who were prepared to walk or ride. From the industrial revolution came the middle classes, better off families who could afford a holiday from time to time but not their own transport – yet. The extension of the railway from Taunton enabled them to travel with ease from London and the Midlands to Dulverton and Minehead and beyond. The tourist industry had started. Much of the early photographer's commissioned work was to take family groups, not sufficient in itself to make a living. The advent of the tourist helped him to do just that. He made postcards – views of pretty cottages and scenes – to sell to the now numerous holiday makers, to postcard companies and to newspapers. Amateur photographers were at work too and between them recorded a pictorial history of Exmoor and its people.

*Martinhoe 20 c. 1910. An unknown photographer using a whole or half plate camera with extending bellows probably of the 1896 to 1904 vintage. Note the black cloth – this excluded the light from behind when he looked through the camera and its lens to compose and focus the subject on the screen at the back before inserting the film. He has an adjustable wooden tripod and uses an air bulb to release the shutter thus eliminating camera shake.*

Families were larger in the earlier 1900s, contraception being virtually unheard of by the working classes. In any event most couples wanted to have large families, grown up children to look after them in their old age. The dread of old people was eviction if they were unable to work and pay rent. Eviction meant the workhouse. Fortunately for Exmoor, the estate owners and landlords were generally of benevolent disposition and old retainers and tenants were usually allowed to live out their lives without disturbance. Skilled artisans hoped that the boys of the family would work with them and learn their trade. Girls stayed at home, went into service or married. The Wootton Courtenay estate of some 2382 acres was owned by Lord Sherborne. The estate, which included the whole village and many farms, was sold in April 1920 in 53 lots largely, we are told, to sitting tenants.

*Wootton Courtenay 28 c. 1925 – perhaps later. The carpenter's house – then Myrtle, now Woodbine Cottage.*
*Mrs James Morgan, the carpenter's wife, and family pictured outside their home – 11 in all including James.*

Neither the blacksmith nor the carpenter would do much work outside the village and the farms around, the big house and the parish church. Indeed their work was limited by the distance they could reasonably walk. It was rare indeed for them to own a horse or pony and trap so income was often limited for lack of transport. Much of their work would demand both skills, thus the smithy was usually close by the carpenter's shop. This close co-operation was necessary if the work was to be done (and was the case in my own hamlet). The village carpenter was very often the undertaker as well and his wife would often do the laying out.

*Wootton Courtenay 26 c. 1910. Wootton Courtenay smithy. In front, third from left, stands Harry Priscott the blacksmith. James Morgan the carpenter is second from right. They worked alongside each other, the smithy being adjacent to the carpenter's shop. In the picture are – at the back – Alf Court (with pickaxe), Mr Phelps, Sam Baker and Jim (Jumbo) Bailey. In front L-R Mrs Priscott (the smith's wife), Bill Smith (his nephew), Harry Priscott (the smith), George Morgan, Harry Roberts, Will Braunten, Mrs Dave Roberts (with Leonard), Mrs Morgan and Nettle, James Morgan (the carpenter) and George Williams.*

Simonsbath is in the parish of Exmoor, one of the 42 parishes in the geographical area encompassed by Exmoor National Park. The fact that the parish bears the same name as the National Park causes confusion and for this reason is referred to, in this book and in the Photographic Archive, as Simonsbath.

Most of its 23 square miles was bought in 1818 by John Knight a wealthy iron-founder from the Midlands who had the idea of turning the empty moorland into a prosperous and populated area by the introduction of cattle and arable farming. He built roads and planted hedges and trees. He ploughed up the moorland and later his son, Frederic, built farm-houses and cottages for tenant farmers and their labourers. The land was poor and many tenant farmers gave up the struggle and went away. The moor was won but at great cost. When Frederic took up the challenge he concentrated on sheep and this proved more successful.

*Simonsbath 30 c. 1910. There are many pictures of Simonsbath but this one best shows the disposition of the hamlet now at the very centre of Exmoor National Park. What is now Simonsbath House Hotel, once the home of John Knight, is in the centre of the landscape. St Luke's, the parish church of Exmoor, can be seen top right.*

Local men used to the hard conditions took over from earlier incoming tenants. Financing the further development of the venture became a problem and in hope of solving it Frederic turned his attention to mineral deposits, but the ore was comparatively poor and transport difficult. The estate was sold to Earl Fortescue and when it was broken up during the latter part of the twentieth century, much of the moorland was purchased for the nation under the management of Exmoor National Park Authority. During the time of the Knight's development the population increased from just one to over 500, when a church was built – a condition of the original purchase – and completed in 1856. Its Golden Jubilee in 1906 was recorded with photographs of the choir and of the congregation. For full details read Roger A. Burton's fascinating book, *Simonsbath: the Inside Story of an Exmoor Village.*

*Simonsbath 7 1906. The choir of St Luke's, the parish church at Simonsbath, at the time of the Rev. H.F.Ramsay.*

The picturesque parish of Selworthy which includes the villages of Allerford and Bossington is never missed by the photographer. The villages lie on the edge of Porlock Vale, a low lying area of Exmoor with land sufficiently fertile to sustain arable farms. Allerford houses the West Somerset Museum of Rural Life in what was once the village school. The Victorian school room has been preserved and is frequently used by teachers to demonstrate to their classes how children were taught, treated and clothed in Victorian times. The museum houses a multitude of artefacts from those used by the skilled craftsman to the domestic, from which one can marvel at our ancestors' ingenuity with the materials then available to them. It also holds many albums of photographs.

*Selworthy 42 1911. Allerford bridge is probably the most illustrated bridge in the Westcountry, popular with photographers and artists alike. This elegant picture from a family album taken in Edwardian times depicts mother and children feeding the ducks.*

*Selworthy 15 1930. Selworthy Green with its thatched cottages is known the country over and everyone with a camera takes a picture. Here we see a Lorna Doone pageant at a most dramatic moment. It has drawn a crowd of over 300 people. Has the Green seen such an occasion before or since?*

*Selworthy 79 1993. Bossington village. Little has changed from a hundred years ago. The tall chimneys – are they to guard the thatch or improve the draught? – are a local feature.*

*Dulverton 131 c. 1885. John German, Dulverton's resident photographer is seated front right in this picture taken in the courtyard in the well of Dulverton's present Guildhall Centre. Back row (from left to right): grandfather William German, Henry German and Lewis German. Middle row: Mrs Bradley, great grandfather Henry German, great grandmother German. Front row: Mrs Arscott and John German, the photographer.*

John German, a professional photographer, worked around Dulverton from c.1880 moving to Paignton in 1920. He started his business in the flat over an ironmonger's shop then owned by the German family. The building, now part of Dulverton's Guildhall Centre, is occupied by the Exmoor National Park Visitor Centre and County Library at the front and the Civic Society's Heritage Centre at the back.

John German's studio was in the building facing the churchyard to the left of the lych gate. At Paignton he and his children developed the business and opened several shops in towns along the south coast at Haywards Heath, Bournemouth and Bognor. Like all the photographers of his day he took family groups and pictures for postcards. He was also commissioned by many of the businesses in the Dulverton area and produced magnificent enlargements which were framed to furnish the walls of the local hotels – have a look on the walls of the Lion Hotel in the town today. Indeed, anything to further his interest and income. Several of his pictures appear on the following pages.

*Dulverton 175 c. 1890. A photograph taken by John German of the Bishop family posing opposite the Lion Hotel. The picture was taken to record the return of a son from the U.S.A. At the top towards the right a map of the U.S.A. can be seen. Was it the son on the extreme right or the one on the left who had returned?*

*Dulverton 72 c.1890. Fore Street Dulverton from Bank Square. The Lion Hotel has no portico and Union Street to the left is a passage to the Lion stable yard, now the Lion car park. The present post office appears to be boarded up and the general store on its left with the bay windows belonged then to a Mr Bedwell. It burnt down c.1920 and was rebuilt becoming Ellerton's Stores, now Doone House Stores. Other than the ironmongers most of the other buildings appear to be residential.*

*Dulverton 144 c. 1910 perhaps. Looking up the High Street from Mill Leat there is not a car in sight. At the far end where the pharmacy is now is a single storey building, once the town gaol, a bank and a grocers. There are several shops and someone appears to be washing the windows of Thorne Bros, the drapers, this side of the Lamb Hotel. On the left is what appears to be the post cart. These were usually very large but light wicker baskets mounted on four wheels which the postman could push easily.*

On asking an inhabitant of Dulverton born in 1900 what was the greatest difference in the town between his youth and ninety years later he said at once, 'The lack of young people' – the town was full of young men working for the hotels and on the estates like Pixton, Hollam and Northmoor and in Dart's livery stables and the like. Allowing for boundary changes, the present population of 1200 is probably much the same as it was ninety years ago but well over half the inhabitants are retired. Young people must commute or move to a larger town for gainful employment, not just the ambitious. Dulverton's shops and services just survive but are very reliant on tourists.

Dulverton has always been a popular base for the tourist as a look at the visitor's book at the Lion – it begins in 1877 – will tell you. Visitors had their say in those days. One guest wrote, 'I only came for two days but it is so hospitable I stayed for two weeks'. Underneath in another hand is written, 'Not wanted at home'. Humour was not lacking.

*Dulverton 69  c. 1910.  Ostlers, grooms, coaches and coachmen; the coaching staff of the Lion Hotel.*

J.H.B. Peel in *Portrait of Exmoor* describes the ancient town of Dunster as 'the fairest on Exmoor' and postcards and pictures depicting Dunster have been produced in their thousands over the years. At this time you could come by train and no doubt by prior arrangement a pony and trap from the Luttrell Arms would pick you up from the station. From this hostelry you could explore the town, once a centre for crafts and trades and all sorts of shops, but now full of cafés and fancy goods.

*Dunster 24 c.1900. The Yarn Market, the Castle and the Luttrell Arms.*

Minehead, while not in Exmoor National Park, has by virtue of its harbour and its visitors contributed much to the development of the Park. As in Dulverton, the advent of the railway in the 1870s brought the tourist and his money and Minehead quickly grew into an affordable popular resort. A guide book of 1904 describes Minehead as 'one of the most pleasant and picturesquely environed watering places of a very lovely coast. Pop. 2500.'

*Minehead 29 1898. Modesty was all when one went bathing in the sea. The bather entered the bathing machine from the door at the back and changed into bathing attire, a shapeless garment that covered the person from neck to ankle; somewhat like combinations but not at all form fitting. The machine was wheeled into the sea until the water level was almost up to the floor. Then the bather opened the front door and by means of steps gently entered the water. There were bathing machines for men and bathing machines for women; never did the sexes mix. On completion of one's swim the machine was used for drying and changing and pushed back up the beach so one could emerge just as one went in and as if nothing had happened. At Minehead as at Lynmouth bathers were segregated; women and girls bathed from the main beach while men and boys swam a quarter of a mile away off Warren Point.*

For the photographer to be able to compare scenes like this is a delight as so often ground cover and building changes prevent it. These two pictures both taken from the second floor of the Overstream Hotel show very clearly how little Porlock has changed over the last 100 years. Can you spot the changes?

The parish of Porlock is an ancient one and the village including West Porlock, Porlock Weir and Hawkcombe has one of the largest populations in Exmoor National Park. It has always been a centre for crafts and trades and its famous hill has both attracted and terrified the tourist. One couple repeating a holiday of long ago asked somewhat nervously at a visitor centre, 'Is the hill still there?' Many of the early cars were neither by virtue of their power able to get up the hill nor by their inefficient brakes able to get safely down it.

*Porlock 20  c.1900.  This view was taken nearly 100 years ago – now look to the right.*

The post in the centre of the picture was once festooned with telephone and electricity cables leading everywhere – an eyesore. Exmoor National Park Authority funded the project to run the cables underground removing them from view. This was a great improvement both for the village and of course the photographer who so often is thwarted by overhead wires.

*Porlock 61  1994.  This same view was taken nearly 100 years later than the one on the left.*

At the beginning of the nineteenth century Lynmouth must have been very isolated and little visited except by those who preferred not to pay duty on their brandy and their baccy. It was a fishing village and the old guide books imply that the villagers lived on herring. By 1831 a number of hotels had been built and the town was soon to become a popular watering place approached by regular stage coach from Porlock or by boat. It is amusing today to note that ladies could only bathe west of the pier and gentlemen half a mile east towards the Foreland. Until 1890 visitors wishing to go to Lynton, 400 feet above, were carried by donkey at 6d. a time. The cliff railway, built by the Jones brothers and operating on a water balance system, opened in 1890 carrying people and cars unable to manage the hills.

*Lynton 80 1831. Lynmouth: an artist's impression taken from an engraving by James Bingley.*

*Lynton 70 c.1900. The cliff railway joining
Lynton with Lynmouth.*

In 1904 passengers paid 2d. to go down and 3d. to go up and 4d. return but it cost 7/6 to have your car taken up to Lynton at a time when average wages were a £1 a week. The cliff railway was a great asset at the time of the disastrous flood in August 1952 rescuing people and cars unable to leave by road. The Barnstaple-Lynton railway opened in 1895 (closed 1935). This must have been a delightful journey and at about 1d. per mile very reasonable. Motor coaches ran from Ilfracombe and the steamer from Bristol cost 3/6 return 5/-. There were several large hotels and it is interesting to note they advertised 'a garage with pit'. Perhaps the chauffeurs spent a lot of the holiday under their employer's car. Another attribute of the villages was electric light which must have made it popular with photographers; a steady light for their enlargers. A hydro electric power station existed in Lynmouth fed by the East Lyn river until washed away in the '52 flood. It was financed by Sir George Newnes, publisher, of Hollerday House as was the Lynton and Barnstaple railway and the Town Hall.

*Exford 7 c.1900. At Exford in 1815 there was just a bridge and a cottage or two. The Knight's venture (see pages 6 and 7) in the mid 1800s created a 'boom town' and the population rapidly increased to several hundred. This picture, copied from a very poor original, gives an idea of the activity on Fair Day – look at all the traps and the people sitting on the bridge. The hotel must have been very busy – hopefully all the ponies knew their way home for it is doubtful whether all their owners did!*

*Winsford 1 1910. The Royal Oak Inn must have been photographed a thousand times or more and the series of pictures in the Archive show the changes that have taken place.*

*Pretty Winsford claims fame with a plaque which reads: 'Ernest Bevin Statesman was born here on 9th March 1881'. He rose from Secretary of the T.G.W.U. to Minister of Labour and National Service during the 1939–45 war (thus 'Bevin Boys') to Secretary of State for Foreign Affairs in 1945.*

*Winsford 38 1900 and below, Wootton Courtenay 23 c. 1880. Drawing water from the stream.*

*The idyll of living in a pretty cottage with roses round the door and hollyhocks down the path is rather spoilt by this more down to earth view. A beaten earth floor, no running water let alone hot and cold, no indoor loo but an earth closet down the garden, no electricity or gas but candles or perhaps an oil lamp for lighting – you probably didn't need light except for emergencies, illness and suchlike, as you worked from sunrise to sunset and were too tired to do anything but go to bed. Cooking – over an open fire – but not much of that, a very basic diet, bread, potatoes, dripping, vegetables grown in the garden, perhaps a bit of jam from a fruit tree, no room for hollyhocks and perhaps a bit of butcher's meat occasionally or with luck a rabbit. Not so good!*

21

*Martinhoe 17 c.1900. Cottage at Kemacott*
*Martinhoe 18 1995. The same cottage*
*re-named Joydale*

Frank Summers, a retired Congregational
Minister born in Oldways End in the early
1900s, has said: 'Life must have been very
hard for our parents and for our grand-
parents. If I could be transported back into
time as it was then, and I could be transported back there as I am now to try and
live there, I simply couldn't. There was no
electricity, no gas of course, no water on
tap and consequently no mod-cons of any
kind. No bathroom, no flush toilets, no
fridge, no Hoover, no washing machine or
spin drier, no drip-dry materials, no
biological washing powder, although there
was powder of a sort (Soako), but washday
was mainly a matter of scrubbing brush,
scrubbing board, household soap and elbow
grease.' 'Thinking of my own home with
my father and grandfather in the smithy,
you can imagine how dirty their shirts
must have got. But then, you see, all work
was that hard. On the farm, for example,
no milking machines and no tractors. It
was a matter of earning a meagre living by
the sweat of the brow. For girls it wasn't
any better. If they weren't kept at home
until their marriage, what could they do
except farm work or what was euphemis-
tically called 'domestic service' – a form of
slavery really most of the time.' Frank's
father and grandfather were skilled men
and his family were comparatively
comfortably off.

*Wootton Courtenay 21   1900.  Allen's Cottages and 25 of the inhabitants.*

*Wootton Courtenay 20  c. 1940.  The same cottages with perhaps 10 or 12 inhabitants. The grown up married children now have their own houses.*

*Brendon 22 1992. Hoar Oak valley. On the left towards the top of the hill are said to be the remains of a Bronze Age settlement, a place of long long ago. The thought comes to mind that it might have been quite an experience to have photographed a group of ancient Britons – if one had survived! In the centre just above the walkers are the remains of a sheep-fold.*

# SECTION TWO
# *Churches and Chapels*

*Minehead 47  c. 1900.  Church Steps.*

When this picture was taken St Mary's, Molland had on its walls framed documents giving instructions of what to do in the event of the invasion expected imminently. No, not 1940 but 1804 when Napoleon was bent on unifying Europe. The villagers are all named and are instructed in which cart they are to flee. Strangely there is no mention of where they are to go or what to do when they get there. It was apparently sufficient that they should have left.

*Molland 9  1979.  St Mary's parish church, Molland.*

*Molland 12  1979.  The three-decker pulpit and sounding board at St Mary's, Molland.*

'We think you have had better weather than we have, it rained all Sunday from 2 o'clock. Monday morning rained until 12 o'clock. Tuesday we went to Doone Valley it rained all the way there but cleared up after, we left here 10.30 arrived there about 1 o'clock. It poured so hard when we got to the Farm house that we could not go to the Valley. The scenery going there is glorious I have never seen anything like it. We came back a different way, you do get a few sensations on the drive what with hills up and down and roundabout roads. Then a lovely drive along the top of the cliffs 1227 feet above sea level. To crown it the driver showed us a place where a motor car went over about 3 weeks ago this is just before you get into Lynmouth which we stopped and went up the Cliff railway to Lynton had a walk round.'

*Oare 6 c.1930. The interior of the church of St Mary at Oare. This picture was copied from a view on a concertina type letter card popular in the 1930s. Under this picture was written in pencil in tiny writing, 'Lorna Doone was married here', so we know that of all the places on the card they did actually visit Oare church. The text of the letter, so typical of an Exmoor holiday then and even now, is given above and overleaf. It is sent by Mum and Dad to Olive, Nellie and Ethel.*

'At 4.30 embarked again another stop at Watersmeet, Dad went down to see it I stopped on top. It is where two waterfalls meet, you see nothing but huge hills valleys and waterfalls nearly all the way on this drive you really must not miss it when you come here it was 9/-. I myself think it was reasonable as we left here at 10.30 arrived back at 6.30 a good day, had hot dinner when we came home. Mrs R. packed us up sandwiches more than we could eat, we get plenty of good food so I am sure you will be alright it is a lovely house. You could get a bus in our bedroom it is so large you can see the sea from the windows, yesterday morning I could see the Welsh coast, if it is fine tomorrow we are going to Cardiff by boat. I get out as much as I can but the hills, oh dear. Much love, Mum and Dad. (Lovely isn't it).'

*Oare 7  c.1930.  The church of St Mary at Oare.  The trees have grown and it is not possible to see this view today.*

*Withypool (and Hawkridge) 31 1992. St Giles, the parish church of Hawkridge, a tiny hamlet overlooking the River Barle and home to the Lock family, carpenters there for over 180 years.*

*Withypool (and Hawkridge) 32  1992.  The belfry at St Giles, Hawkridge shortly after the carriage was restored and the bells rehung with help from amongst others the Exmoor National Park Authority.*

*Luccombe 60 before 1910. The lych gate and tower of St Mary's, the parish church of Luccombe as photographed by Francis Frith. Frith was a famous photographer of his day, much travelled and many of his pictures, for instance of his journeys in Egypt, are sought to illustrate books. Churches were a very popular subject at the time and tourists might well spend a whole holiday examining each one within easy reach and of course buying the postcard views.*

*Porlock 64  before 1896.  Culbone church, dating from the 1200s, claims to be the smallest parish church in England.  It can only be reached by a footpath which has, from time to time, been brought further inland as erosion has destroyed the cliff edge that it ran along originally.  An early photograph by Francis Frith.*

Dulverton currently has three churches, the Congregational, whose members are portrayed here, a Roman Catholic and a traditional Anglican church built on an eminence at the top of the town. All, for these days, are well supported although comparing the number of children in the pictures then and now bodes ill for the future. It seems that every village on Exmoor, however small, has its own church and indeed in earlier times the parson and the squire were a useful check and balance one on the other so that neither could dominate their village to their own ends. The parson was concerned with the practical as well as the spiritual welfare of the villagers, caring for the poor, the sick and the aged.

To an extent this role was shared with the squire and the general welfare of the village could depend upon their co-operation or rivalry. Often the parson was so poor himself that money and the getting of it took up much of his time and many had sidelines ranging from minor trades to pupils and perhaps a cut from smugglers for the use of tombs for storage!

*Dulverton 155 1931. A centenary photograph of members of Dulverton Congregational Church. There are some 87 people in the picture including 35 children or so. Many people worshipped at the non-conformist chapels because they felt that the parish church was for the 'toffs'.*

Today the role and influence of the village parson has been reduced by the advent of the welfare state and for many going to church is not so important. The parson often serves several parishes and is no longer part of the village, a village in which the population is continually changing. Where are his roots? None the less there is yet some strength but as time goes on it seems possible that some of the village churches will go the way of the school and the shop.

*Dulverton 157  1981.  The 150th anniversary photograph of Dulverton Congregational Church, with members seen outside their chapel in Millhams Lane.   The picture includes 37 people, amongst them six children.*

Dulverton can boast two famous sons. One of these was George Hall Peppin who with his wife Harriet and two sons George and Frederick lived at Old Shute Farm from 1823. Things did not go well. In 1850 the family went to Australia where after appalling trials and tribulations he bred the Merino sheep of generous fleece and able to withstand the climate. This breed is now common not only in Australia but in South Africa and South America. He made nothing out of his efforts and one notes with interest that at the end of each month when he did his accounts his diary contains the note 'opened a case of gin'. Daresay he needed it. The whole story is told in the book *The Sturdy Breed* by Steven Pugsley.

Sir George Williams, born at Ashway Farm went to London as a young man of twenty-one and became a draper. Of strong Christian faith he was instrumental in the founding of the Y.M.C.A. in 1841. He was a skilful business man and when he died in 1905 left £250,000. He is buried in St Paul's Cathedral and there is a window in his memory in Westminster Abbey.

*Dulverton 60 c.1920. All Saints, the parish church of Dulverton. On the left is the magnificent sycamore tree of which only the stump now remains. The dedication 'All Saints' was often used when it was felt that the local population needed the help of all the saints. One wonders whether this was so here!*

*Dulverton 161 1994. One of the George Williams' windows in memory of the founder of the Y.M.C.A.*

*Old Cleeve 36 1989. Part of the chapter house at Cleeve Abbey, a Cistercian monastery, founded in 1198. The lands were extensive and included parts of Roadwater, Bilbrook, Withycombe and Luxborough as well as holdings in Devon and Cornwall. Despite the fact that it was an extremely charitable institution the Abbey was dissolved in 1537. One of the monks became Bishop of Gloucester in 1551, but on the accession of Queen Mary he was taken, tried, and condemned as an obstinate heretic and burned at the stake in Gloucester in 1555 'for the example and terror of others'. The chapter house was the meeting place of the monks where the Abbot or Subprior might instruct or discuss matters with the brothers. Although the eastern end no longer exists, it can strike one as being extraordinarily draughty and uncomfortable; but then perhaps no-one wanted to prolong any discussion, a lesson of which many committees would do well to take notice.*

# SECTION THREE
# Schools and Schooling

*Wootton Courtenay 8 c. 1910. The Sunday School outing – the reward for regular attendance over the past year.*
*All wonderfully clean and tidy in their best clothes – where did they go in the horse and cart? At Oldways End, Sunday School*
*was at 10.15 am followed by a morning service at 11 am. In the afternoon Sunday School was at 1.45 pm followed in the*
*winter by a service a 2.30 pm and in the summer at 6.30 pm.*

Attendance at school became compulsory in 1870 and by 1880 free education up to the age of thirteen became available to all. Nearly every village had its own school, some provided by local gentry, some by the Church and some by the voluntary efforts of the villagers themselves. In 1902 faceless authorities took control, arbitrarily setting dates etc. on a national basis. These regulations were resented by the villages as no account was taken of the demands of harvesting etc. and so were generally ignored. In the old school registers at West Anstey there was the column 'occupation' against each name – farm labourer, shepherd etc. In the column for non-attendance were the reasons – busy at home, harvesting, lambing etc. Teacher(s) would concentrate on the 'three Rs' adding in a little history, geography and basic science for the older children with perhaps some practical domestic science and handicrafts. That sounds very sensible but often there was only one teacher for the five to fourteen-year-olds, no equipment to speak of other than a blackboard, slates and pencils, and cold and uncomfortable school-rooms.

*West Anstey 6  c.1935.  A group taken at the front of the school some years before it closed and became a private house into which the last head teacher, Mrs L. Wilkins, retired.*

Frank Summers was asked what the children did in their spare time when they weren't at school and had finished their homework and any household jobs like blackleading the stove or setting the kindling ready under the copper. He commented, 'Children today can't understand a world that had no record players, no television, no wireless. Of course we didn't even have a cinema. Like our elders, we had to make our own amusements. Outdoors we had hoops guided by an iron crook made in the smithy. We had games like marbles, especially valuing the ginger beer ones, but they were scarce because you had to smash the bottle. (There was a returnable deposit). Indoors there were the usual games. There seemed to be more family life then. Parents didn't have those other attractions like TV and would find time to play games with us, perhaps draughts or dominoes. Reading was encouraged. On Sunday after evening service we would walk to the main road and watch the traffic speeding along at a very dangerous rate – it must have been at least at 40 mph.'

*East Anstey 26 1922. A group taken at the back of what is now East Anstey Primary School.*
*In 1922 the school taught pupils up to the school leaving age of fourteen. Frank Summers who is quoted*
*on page 22 and above can be seen third from the left in the back row.*

This letter was written to Mrs J. Ball of Wootton Courtenay who over the years has amassed photographs and data relating to the history of the village. Florence Baker M.R.S.T. writes about her first visit to Wootton Courtenay and her experiences as the head teacher. 'On a bright April morning in 1920 I arrived at Dunster Station for an interview with the Rector with regard to the headship of Wootton Courtenay Church School. A gentleman met me and drove me to the Rectory. On alighting I was taken into the drawing room, to discover the gentleman was the Rector himself, which amused him greatly. We soon got down to business and afterwards I was taken to see the school premises, and then back to the Rectory for refreshments. The drive to and from the station was most delightful, I was so taken with the scenery. Needless to say, I was pleased to learn I had obtained the appointment.'

*Wootton Courtenay 4  1893.  A school group of over 70 pupils.*

*Wootton Courtenay 5  c.1930.  A school group of over 40 pupils.*

'It was a two teacher school, and the infant teacher already lived in the village. In a very short time, however, she left to get married and my sister filled the vacancy. We found the children eager to learn and the first pupil to pass the entrance test to a Grammar School was Muriel Conibere who chose Bishop Fox's at Taunton. Her success was followed periodically by four other pupils, Hester Taplin, Robert and Jack Reed, Bessie Quick, all of whom went to Minehead. Cookery lessons were introduced for the girls, and the Instructor was very impressed by their good behaviour and concentration. The years passed very smoothly, until numbers were so low, it became a one teacher post only, and eventually an uncertificated post in the 1930s.' The school closed in 1946 and the ten children remaining were bussed to Timberscombe.

*Wootton Courtenay 7 1946. The last school group; the number of pupils has dropped to ten (one is away). The school closed shortly after this picture was taken.*

Winsford School lasted a great deal longer than either West Anstey or Wootton Courtenay schools and those in many other of the Exmoor villages but gradually the number of pupils fell to the point where the local authority felt it was uneconomical to keep it open despite the opposition of the villagers. In 1918 the school-leaving age was raised to fourteen and until after the 1939-45 war, children would stay at the one school until they were fourteen unless they won a place at the grammar school or were privately educated. Today pupils leave the 'First' or 'Primary' school at nine or eleven and are bussed or taken to the larger unit in a town which has specialist teachers and more equipment. The drop in numbers of school pupils was due partly to the shift of population away from the countryside; a long-term result of the industrial revolution of the 1800s which led to the production of agricultural machinery – mechanical aids for the farm. As machinery was introduced so the labour requirement was reduced. During both World Wars the use of machinery was encouraged to increase home production and free labour for the armed forces. Now many farms are operated by one man, the farmer, with occasional help from an agricultural contractor.

*Winsford 5 1910. A school group showing some 60 pupils and two teachers. Photographers were very keen to take school groups; they always hoped that each child's family would want to buy a print.*

As the farm horse was replaced by the tractor so was the horse drawn cart and carriage by the lorry and car. Thus the Lion in Dulverton could replace 20 ostlers and grooms with one car and a driver. The net result was a drop in population as many young people moved to the towns to get work in the factories. As the young people moved away so the numbers of children fell. The drop in population of the Exmoor villages was quite dramatic and did not level off until the 1930s. These school groups tell in pictures part of the story.

*Winsford 6 1993. A school group of 20 pupils and three teachers taken shortly before the school closed.*

*Dulverton 215  1994.  A very different school.  National Park Ranger Tim Braund teaching children (and a parent or two) about the countryside and its care.  This picture was taken during the Woodland Craft Week, part of Exmoor National Park's celebration of its 40th birthday.  Exmoor National Park Authority takes its responsibility of educating young people very seriously, helping not only local school children but also those from other parts of the UK and from other countries.  They help those seeking Duke of Edinburgh awards and run both day and residential courses at the Pinkery Centre.*

# SECTION FOUR
# *Work on the Farm*

*Minehead Without 5  c. 1910.  Wonderful cream teas were served at Greenaleigh Farm for years.
In the foreground are Alice, Ada and Lily Rawle.*

*Simonsbath 63  c.1930.  A fine Exmoor Horn ram, typical of the native breed that can be seen all over Exmoor National Park and whose population far exceeds that of us humans.  For the full story of sheep ranching on Exmoor read* Exmoor 40 Years On *by Hilary Binding.*

*Winsford 8  1989.  Ewes and lambs at Liscombe at the time of the experimental farm.*

*Simonsbath 8 c.1980. This picture is of Nos 1, 2 and 3 West Cottages on the Challacombe road out of Simonsbath. They were originally built by the Knights as steam engine sheds and were later converted to three cottages. Some time later when the old mortar was dug out of the walls preparatory to re-pointing, the two archways through which the steam engines passed in and out of the sheds could be clearly seen. The small blocked up aperture seen over the main arch was made to allow for the height of the spark arrester. This device was an extension to the engine chimney and fitted to stop sparks flying out and setting the thatched roof on fire. Once outside the shed the arrester could be removed.*

*Old Cleeve 27 c.1920. An ancient traction engine of the type that would have been housed in the original sheds shown on page 50. When the Knights first started their venture of quickly bringing prosperity to the so-called waste of Exmoor, they broke up the ground using plough teams of six bullocks. Later the Knights introduced steam ploughing engines. These were used in pairs, one on each side of the field, with a heavy flexible wire attached to the rotating drum under each engine. To this wire, plough blades were fitted so arranged that the plough would operate in either direction. From one engine the wire was slowly drawn in and slowly released from the other so as to maintain tension. In this way the heaviest land could be turned over ready for tilling. Engines of this type were used for breaking heavy virgin ground up to and including the 1939-45 war. Today they can often be seen at steam engine rallies.*

*Simonsbath 52  c.1905.  Sheep must be well looked after and shepherding is an important job.  As well as tending and protecting the flock the shepherds would all have joined in the annual task of shearing.  In the picture standing from left to right are: Jim Little, John Jones, labourer, Archie Jackson, Hoar Oak shepherd, John Little, Pinkery shepherd, Robert Little, Limecombe and head shepherd, William Little jnr, Larkbarrow shepherd, William Little snr, Toms Hill shepherd, Willy Blythe, Badgworthy shepherd, and Lady Fortescue, wife of Lord Fortescue, then owner of the estate.  Sitting, left to right: a friend of the Fortescue family, Tommy Little, Limecombe shepherd, William Bain, mines shepherd, William Welch, marker boy, unknown, and Richard Jones, labourer.*

*Wootton Courtenay 43  c.1930.  Jack Reed of Wootton Courtenay shearing sheep.  This must have been very hard on the hands, the back and the knees.  The shears, rather like a heavy pair of scissors with wide blades, are in his right hand.  Behind him are sheep awaiting their turn; a bit like a visit to the dentist for us one suspects.  The shearer's art was to be able to cut off the fleece neatly in one piece without nicking the sheep.  The fleeces were taken to market and sold for making wool.*
*The Exmoor National Park visitor centre displays at Dunster tell the complete story from the sheep to the finished cloth.*

*Withypool (and Hawkridge) 2 c.1930. A flock of sheep passing by the Royal Oak at Withypool perhaps on their way to market. Today one thinks only of young lambs going to market but from earliest times up until the late 1940s we used to eat mutton, sheep meat from older animals and very good it was too, especially cold with home made chutney. Perhaps because it was cheap, it tended to be looked down upon and for various reasons it became the practice to only eat the younger lamb. In these days of freezers a whole mutton takes up little room and with the help of a co-operative butcher one can enjoy a pleasant change in diet.*

*The Royal Oak looks very different today and one is intrigued by the flight of stairs on the outside of the building. A picture taken at a similar time shows a doorway at the top leading into the building, a meeting room some say. There are no signs of it having been bricked up and the stairs look as if they have been there for some while. A little mystery which no doubt someone will clear up.*

*Winsford 20  c.1925.  On the alert at Edbrooke Farm.  A good dog, or two or three, was essential for the old time shepherd not only to help him control and guard the flock but also to keep him company in his lonely hut up on the moor. What better than the border collie, that most intelligent of dogs, which is found on most farms today.*

*Winsford 12  1908.  Market day at Winsford.  Most villages had their markets then, even the smaller ones like East and West Anstey, but most have closed.  Cutcombe market is probably the largest and the best attended today.*

*Exford 33 1957. The market at Exford held in what was called the auction field where Exmoor National Park Authority now have their depot. In the foreground, no doubt holding forth on matters of the day, is Sir Edward DuCann, for many years M.P. for Taunton.*

Once a year often on Lady Day, 25 March, estate tenants would pay their dues. They wore their best clothes to keep up appearances. No-one was going to admit to doing badly. The estate steward would sit at a table in a room like the one at Court House at North Molton, the tenants standing at the far end. They came forward as their names were called. The table was often a drum table, one made with a revolving top with drawers underneath.

*Simonsbath 64 1927. George VI when Duke of York inspecting prize Exmoor Horns at Spitalfields Market in London. (This picture and the one of the ram on page 48, reproduced by courtesy of the Exmoor Horn Sheep Society, are included in the Simonsbath collection for convenience.)*

The tenant sitting opposite the steward, opened the drawer in front of him and placed in it the rent money in a small bag and the rent book. The table would be turned until the drawer was opposite the steward who would open it, count the money and returning it to the bag place it in an adjacent drawer which he would lock. The steward would receipt the rent book and return the table to its original position for the tenant to take and leave. The next tenant called would then come forward and the process would continue. In this way no-one except the steward knew the amount of the rent. This was to prevent any tenant knowing what another paid. It kept the peace, for favouritism for one reason or another was not unknown and it enabled the landlord and the favoured tenant to keep their secret. Whether this was the practice at Court House we do not know, but it was a common custom at the time when coin of the realm was used for most transactions.

*North Molton 8 c.1900. Tenants on the Poltimore Estate outside Court House on Rent Day.*

Farming on Exmoor has always been hard and traditionally the farmer's wife has played her part, anything from looking after the poultry and bringing up orphan lambs to helping with milking as well as bringing up the children. Many did and do more than this becoming expert in the dairy and making butter and cheese and marketing it themselves.

Some women are successful farmers in their own right and can plough or do any other job as well as any man. In the book *English Villages* by Valerie Porter, one of the best on the subject, she mentions a very good plough-woman who unfortunately fell pregnant when employed as an under-carter – the head carter took his role too literally.

*Winsford 55 c.1930. Bottle feeding a lamb at Edbrooke Farm. (Mrs F. Jenkins who was brought up on Edbrooke Farm provided the Exmoor Photographic Archive with many pictures of life on the farm taken for and by her parents Mr and Mrs Bale.)*

*Wootton Courtenay 37 c.1950. Feeding the poultry at Brookside Farm. (The lady in the picture is the mother of Mr J. Ball who farmed at Brookside for many years.)*

*Selworthy 5  c.1915.  Mr Staddon of Selworthy cutting grass with a scythe of the type used for haymaking.  A reaping hook was used for cutting corn.*

Photographs of actual work on the Exmoor farm are few and far between. There was little in it for the professional photographer and the farmer's family were much too busy to be taking photographs until harvesting was complete. So it tended to be left to the interested amateur and thankfully there were a few about.

Agricultural machinery came very late to Exmoor. It was difficult to make ends meet and there was little capital available for such investments. None the less, those who did invest soon found that savings were quickly made. Thus on one farm of some 300 acres, one reads of the purchase of a reaping machine like the one illustrated below. It cost about £35 in 1890 and was operated by two men. When harvest time came the farmer found that the machine and its two operators could do the same amount of work in the time that it took 16 men with scythes. He reckoned it saved him 4/- an acre – £60!

*Molland 3 1940. Bill Buckingham reaping at Pulworthy Farm. The same type of horse-drawn reaping machine that first came out in the 1870s or so, but no doubt with some improvements, was still in use after seventy years.*

## THE FARMER

The farmer will never be happy again,
He carries his heart in his boots,
For either the rain is destroying his grain
Or the drought is destroying his roots.

*Parracombe 5 c.1930. The sheaves thrown out by the reaping machine on the previous page have been gathered and stacked vertically, several at a time, into stooks. Hopefully any rains will run off and the wind and sun will dry them out before threshing.*

In fact if you meet this unfortunate man
The conclusion is only too plain
That nature is just an elaborate plan
To annoy him again and again

*Brompton Regis 15  c.1900.  Gupworthy Farm at Withiel Florey.  The family poses for the picture. Note the cartload of roots.*

*Wootton Courtenay 46 c.1925. The threshing team. The steam traction engine on the left drove, by means of a belt (the diagonal line behind and either side of the chimney), the wooden threshing machine on the right. The sheaves of wheat, barley etc brought by cart from the field were fed into this machine where they were threshed or beaten. The purpose was to separate the seeds of the plant, the grain, from the straw and husks. The grain was funnelled out into sacks for use as seed for next year or to be ground into meal for animal feed or flour. The straw, the stalks, was collected and used for bedding livestock. Gradually this system of harvesting was superseded by the combine harvester which did the whole job of reaping, threshing and so forth in the field but these were very expensive and on Exmoor farms of small acreages a farmer was more likely to hire one than to buy one.*

*Selworthy 72 c.1920. Haymaking. The grass has grown tall and ripened in the sun. It has been cut, perhaps by scythe or horse drawn grass cutter, and the horse rake on the right is gathering it up ready to load onto the carts. It is then taken to the place where the farmer has decided to site his haystacks (see over) and later used as winter feed for his sheep, cattle and horses. This was an essential part of being self sufficient. Too little hay and the farmer had to buy at a price. Today the whole job is done in the field, the grass is either cut green for silage or ripe when it is baled; the purpose is the same, for feed.*

*Dunster 7 c.1930. The haymaking has been done, time now for a group photograph to record the event for the family album. Note the size of the colossal haystack. It was very important that the hay be quite dry. Too moist and it would start to ferment, get hot and catch fire – spontaneous combustion it was called. The ladders are very long, imagine how hard it was to throw the hay up to that height with a pitch fork. The old boy on the right holding the rake seems to have lost a few teeth – the rake's teeth, not his!*

*Parracombe 6 c.1930. The cycle of ploughing, tilling, sowing and harvesting starts all over again. One is reminded of the last line of an old hymn which translated from the Latin proclaims, ' Man sows, man tends, but God gives life'. How true for the farmer and in the broadest sense for all of us.*

*Luccombe 58  1899.  Cloutsham Farm, very photogenic and much visited by tourists at the turn of the century. Several postcards and letters tell us that people were entertained to tea on the lawn.*

# SECTION FIVE

# *Sport and Recreation*

*Withypool (and Hawkridge) 15  1982.  HRH the Prince of Wales joins an invitation meet at Zeal Farm, Hawkridge.*

Hunting in one form or another has always been traditional on Exmoor. To some it is a sport. To others it is a necessity, a way of reducing the rampages of deer on the crops and the murder of lambs and poultry on the farm. Others hate it. Many believe that the staghounds cull the old and the lame and maintain a healthy balance and the foxhounds reduce the number of foxes that would otherwise breed in intolerable numbers. Whether this could be sensibly done by any other means is open to question. Time will tell. What it does do is to bring employment – the hunt staff, livery stables, saddlers and blacksmiths amongst others.

*Nettlecombe 3 c.1955. A meet at Nettlecombe Court. (Details of the meet on this page and that on the next are to date unknown).*

There are few early, turn of the century, pictures of the hunt in the field as this was outside the scope of film at the time. However, it could be managed, and the Photographic Archive would be strengthened should any ever come to light.

*North Molton 9 c.1910. A meet in North Molton Square.*

*Dunster 59  1923.  Playing polo on Dunster Castle Lawns.  Polo was being played at Dunster in the 1890s, perhaps before.  Players came from far and wide including Rajahs and Maharajahs from the Indian states where the sport originated.  In the days without radio and television it was a popular spectator sport.*

On a postcard of Dunster Castle lawns sent to a friend in Sidcup, Kent in 1913 is this message from Allie who was staying at Carhampton Vicarage. 'We are enjoying a thoroughly good wild time. They play polo on a part of the ground on this card. It is just glorious to watch, all County players and only costs 6d. to go in and see it. We are spending all our spare cash on going there. I am absolutely crazy on the game and also on some of the players. Much love Allie'.

*Dunster 54 1923. A formal photograph of the two teams.*

*Luccombe 22  c.1950.  A quiet hack in one of Luccombe's lovely lanes, a timeless pleasure.*

*Minehead 22  c.1895.  There were regular horse races along Minehead beach until about 1898.  The vast crowd must have come from villages all around and of course from the holiday makers who were beginning to visit Minehead in large numbers.*

*Old Cleeve 46 c.1895. An outing from Washford according to the sign on the left. What was it all about? Where were all these people going? Other than a St George's flag, there is nothing to give us a clue. There was no church at Washford until 1910. Perhaps it was a Methodist outing, the chapel here being one of the largest in the area.*

*Dulverton 110 c.1920. An outing with a purpose – picking whorts or more commonly bilberries or whimberries – (like many things the name depends on where you live). This was a definite must for many families providing an additional and useful change in diet at no cost; whortleberry pies and tarts. Very good too. It also provided additional income. Picking them could be a tedious backbreaking occupation and there was a comb made of wood with long teeth which could be run through the plant to speed up the process. There is a fine example in the West Somerset Museum of Rural Life at Allerford amongst all the other ingenious devices of long ago.*

The importance of the tourist and holiday maker to Exmoor cannot be over emphasised. It was indeed fortunate that the railway arrived at the same time that the farmer started to use the new agricultural and other machinery. As the indigenous working population fell the number of visitors to Exmoor rapidly increased and shops and services responded by supplying their needs. Without the tourist many more shops and services would have gone for ever. Locals grumble about the prices and lack of variety in local shops but few use them. People grumble about lack of public transport but when provided never use it. But are these facilities really wanted? The population has changed.

*Combe Martin 2 c.1933. This picture of Newberry Beach was copied from a post card sent by a couple staying in Combe Martin and addressed to a lady in Hounslow, Middlesex. The card reads: 'Wednesday – Dear Ethel, Having a lovely time here – we like the place very much. Went for a motor boat trip round the coast the other evening. Oh! Never again! I can still feel the boat rocking! We are just going to Clovelly, love, Else'. (One can sympathise.)*

A large proportion are retired and out of town shopping is a pleasure, passes the time and is much easier, no parking worries and not too far to carry things. Personal transport is everyone's first ambition anyway as well as a necessity in a rural area. The car brought with it the petrol station and repair shop. Piped water supplies brought the plumber and electric power the electrician. Thus many who might once have been destined to work on the land now work in the service industries. Those employed in the service industries plus the incoming professions, accountants, local government employees, the estate agent and the retired, together help to compensate for the drop in population caused by changes in agricultural practices.

THE SEA WALL, MINEHEAD

*Minehead 7 c.1950. The arrival of the railway made Minehead a popular holiday spot. For many years there was a direct train from Wolverhampton every Saturday making for easy travelling from the Midlands. A postcard of the time sent by one young man staying at a guest house in Minehead to his friend in London includes the comment 'very nice apartment and very obliging landlady, nice looking etc.'. One wonders about the 'etc.'!*

*Luccombe 50  1911.  An Edwardian picnic near Webber's Post.*

*Luccombe 18  c. 1950.  A picnic in Horner Wood.*

*Lynton 57 c.1955. A walk along North Walk to the Valley of Rocks. Pity that the valley has such a massive car park.*

*Luccombe 16 1939. Percy Hutchinson F.R.P.S. of Taunton took this picture of his wife on the clam bridge at Horner. He took many pictures in this style, full of light and shade and as one looks at them one wonders whether he was trying to capture some last moments of peace as the storm clouds gathered.*

CREAM &
PLAIN TEAS.

*Luccombe 2  1950.  Horner Tea Gardens.  After an outing or laze on the beach or walk in this peaceful place of Exmoor, this place where time passes slowly, spiritually refreshed, what better than to refresh ourselves in body too.*

Some looking at this peaceful scene would see it as a waste of space only fit for development such as the erection of so-called executive housing from which they would derive much money. Unfortunately this is not an uncommon view and if it were not for the National Parks much of what is left of the lovely areas of our countryside would have been despoiled.

Over the years one has seen at close hand much of Exmoor National Park Authority's balancing act, furthering the interest of those that live and work on the moor, making provision for visitors who wish to enjoy it but expect all facilities, and at the same time managing to protect this area of natural beauty. So many factors make the Authority's job indeed a mile wide and an inch deep. They are helped in many ways by the Exmoor Society, a surprisingly powerful group, albeit dare one say a bit over protective at times – but no bad thing, who are often able to apply pressure where the Park Authority cannot. Without the one with the help of the other we would not be able to enjoy the Exmoor National Park we see today.

*Exton 2 1940. Bridgetown. Mrs Sampson with Allen and Sheila (who told us about this picture) and their dog Twilight in the peace of the Exe Valley – a part of England's green and pleasant land!*